*A Spiritual Exercise*
*for New Parents*

# *A Spiritual Exercise for New Parents*

ELWYN A. SMITH

Fortress Press        Philadelphia

Copyright © 1986 by Fortress Press

**Library of Congress Cataloging-in-Publication Data**

Smith, Elwyn A. (Elwyn Allen), 1919-

A spiritual exercise for new parents.

1. Parents — Religious life. 2. Spiritual life.
I. Title.
BV4845.S64 1986     242'.64     85-47714
ISBN 0-8006-1863-7

1713F85   Printed in the United States of America   1-1863

In Love and Joy
this book is dedicated to
Patrick and Rebecca Gerlach
Molly Charlotte
born October 27, 1983
and Christopher David
born May 9, 1985

# Contents

# A Spiritual Exercise

A regimen of spiritual exercise is as difficult for the modern person to introduce into the routines of daily life as is regular physical exercise. Perhaps we may take a leaf from the runners' book. Some run to improve their bodies; others are preparing to race; many speak of a general sense of well-being. But to get started, every single one had to make a break with the past.

The birth of a child, particularly the first, demolishes previous routines. But it is not only routines that change when a baby is born – people change. Fundamental questions about life no longer seem merely theoretical. "What should we teach this child? What values really count for us?"

Parenthood, in short, launches us on a new course of personal growth. This book is written for young people who are aware of what is happening. It puts in their hands a guide and aid to their spiritual development.

Like all exercise, spiritual exercise is progressive. This book develops a series of themes appropriate to the evolving experience of new parents. These themes are central to all Christian life; here they unfold in relation to parental experience. Each deals with both God and human feelings, bringing the two together. Since every couple's experience is unique, the themes may be used in whatever order best serves.

Young people who are striving to establish a Christian family order are invited by this book to put the spiritual life at its center. The prayers, adorations, and Scriptures may be used repeatedly. They yield fresh meaning as our experience of life grows.

# How to
# Use This Book

There is perhaps no busier time in the life of a young woman than the first weeks after the birth of her child. New fathers are learning to share responsibility for the care of an infant. Parents who are raising several children have survived the disruptions of the arrival of their firstborn but daily life is still a circus. Time for personal concerns is hard to find.

Yet there is no time of life when the calm and healing of quietness are more needed than in these early years of family life. Time when a husband and wife can be together without distraction is vital. But how to find it!

This little book does not solve that problem; in fact, it will never be used unless parents are working to save some time for themselves. Once a couple has begun to look for ways to do that, this book can help.

The best time to begin to use this book is just before the birth of the baby. Even if this is a first child, the young woman already is a mother, her husband already a father, to the unborn. To begin to think as parents during these months is to be all the more ready for the great changes that come when the baby is born.

It is harder, though, to find time to meet personal needs during the months that follow the birth. The mother of a newborn is usually up at night and sleeping during the day to catch up on her rest. She may have a moment to herself in the morning before the baby awakens. Six weeks later the baby's sleep habits may have changed and private time must be sought at another time of the day.

Similarly with time together. Parents often postpone household work until children are in bed — and this can prevent private time. Yet if parents are seeking time with each other, it is probably best found in the evening.

These spiritual exercises are adaptable. Each day's experience of prayer, adoration, and reflection on the Scripture is built around a theme and is divided into three parts: *Morning*, *Midday*, and *Evening*.

*Morning* is written to be read and used either alone or with one another. The new mother may read it and pray a few minutes before her baby awakens or while she is nursing. For the parent employed outside the home, this book is sized for purse or pocket in order to go to the workplace. It may be read at a coffee break or in the moments of quiet that more and more workers are introducing into their schedules to offset the nerve straining effect of uninterrupted workflow. *Midday* is similarly adaptable.

*Evening*, while suited to the single parent, aims to bring father and mother together. If the day is allowed to pass without this, communication can wither. Feelings not readily dealt with on a daily basis can accumulate until substantial problems develop. *Evening* ideas invite discussion.

# DAY ONE
# *Gratitude*

## MORNING

### Adoration

Sing to the Lord, for he has done glorious things;
let this be known to all the world. Shout aloud and
sing for joy . . . for great is the Holy One of Israel.

(Isa. 12:5, 6, NIV)

### A Thought to Remember

We feel gratitude to many people during the
months before a baby is born: the doctors who
care for us, the parents who pray for us, the friends
who reassure us. We are grateful that a mother's
body is capable of bringing a baby to full term and
that science protects her from many dangers.

We are excited by the progress of science, genetic
engineering, for example, which puts so many
possibilities within human reach. As our power to
control grows, we are more and more engrossed by

technique and may think less about meaning — until something we cannot control, something that we do not understand, breaks abruptly into our lives.

The mother of Jesus had never heard of genes and chromosomes so perhaps it came more easily to her to sing the praises of God after Jesus was born. Yet the beginnings of life still stir a sense of mystery within us. Science does not reach to the deepest questions; there is a wholeness here that lies beyond science. We return, if we are believers, to the great cause, the director of all, and with Mary we praise God, saying: "The Mighty One has done great things for me — Holy is his Name."

## A Prayer of Gratitude

Dear God, we thank you for inviting us to be children in your family. We thank you that Jesus has taught us to call you "Father" and that he is our brother. We are not strong or wise enough to bear responsibility for our child (children) without you and we are grateful for your promise that your Son will walk beside us every day. Help us to hear your Word. Through Jesus we pray. Amen.

# MIDDAY

## A Reflection on Gratitude

There are moments in human experience when the spirit that is open to reality spontaneously feels gratitude. To be sure, many persons lack that openness. Perhaps they feel cheated by life; to them the good things that happen to them are no more than they deserve. Or they may take everything good for granted so that they do not grasp the great goodness of such familiar things as warm shelter, nourishing food, and the birth of a child.

The birth of a child tests the kind of persons we are. Do we feel gratitude? There is much stress and pain involved in pregnancy and childbirth; and the constant care of a small child challenges the self-concern of parents. A first baby in particular creates a sudden demand on parents for rapid personal growth.

To the believer in God, the most fundamental response to all these joys and stresses is gratitude. The desert experience taught the Hebrews what reality was like. After much deprivation, the psalmist praised God for his gifts to his people: hearing their prayers, sustaining their lives, teaching his law. He was open to God. So also was Mary. She is a model of parenthood to this day for her spontaneous song of gratitude for God's great goodness to her.

### The Scriptures

Psalm 65. The psalmist rejoices in gratitude to God.

Luke 1:46–55. Jesus' mother sings her praise of God.

## A Prayer for the Hour

Heavenly Father, we confess that we have not reflected very deeply on how things are with us. We have taken your gifts for granted. We have not thanked you for them and we have been angry when our expectations were disappointed. Help us to make a new beginning. We ask you to accept our thanks through Jesus our Lord. Amen.

# EVENING

## A Theme for Meditation

Since my youth, O God, you have taught me, and to this day I declare your marvelous deeds.

(Ps. 71:17 NIV)

In ancient Israel every individual was surrounded by a family. Family included not only parents and children but relatives of all degrees, servants, visitors, and even total strangers who had asked hospitality. No one could survive alone.

In our culture, by contrast, individualism is extolled everywhere. To do a great deed unaided excites the imagination, as the earliest astronauts who entered space alone or sailors who cross the Atlantic Ocean single-handedly prove. The truth is that almost all modern enterprises are conducted by teams, sometimes numbering in the thousands. We are still deeply formed by family — except that now it consists of technical and professional "kinfolk" rather than a blood-related clan. The family as we know it today — parents and children — has been reduced in scale and has greatly lost its influence on the formation of our youth.

Because little or nothing of God is taught in the modern communities of work, we are thrown largely on our own resources regarding religion. So we join the family of believers by allying ourselves with like-minded people with whom we may worship, study, and pray.

## A Prayer for the Night

Be present with us, loving Father, and bind us together with the whole family of your faithful people. We pray for all parents tonight, whether their children are very young or passing through the difficulties of youth. Help us to choose ways that honor your holy Name and go with us wherever we may go. Through Christ Jesus our Lord. Amen.

# DAY TWO
## *Anxiety*

## MORNING

### Adoration

Shout with joy to God, all the earth! Sing to the glory of his Name! . . . He has preserved our lives and kept our feet from slipping. . . . Praise be to God, who has not withheld his love from us!

(Ps. 45, NIV adapted)

### A Thought To Remember

The desperation of Jairus, the synagogue leader who came to Jesus for help for his very sick daughter, stands in the forefront of Luke's story of the healing of the child. This father's situation speaks to the pervasive problem of human anxiety and in particular to the anxieties of parents.

To Jairus, Jesus responded simply: "Don't be

afraid; just believe" and he healed the child. The healing is Christ's sign to us that in the kingdom of God faith and confidence rule.

Still, anxiety is never banished. Both Scripture and human experience testify to its universality. We know very well how it undercuts joy and stunts creative living. Against this disturbing assault on our existence Jesus speaks very plainly! "Don't be afraid; just believe."

### A Prayer for Trust in God

Heavenly Father, we are often anxious and need to hear your comforting Word. It troubles us when we do not understand why we feel as we do. We ask you to give us confidence in caring for our baby and for each other. Help us to understand you so we may know ourselves through Jesus our Lord. Amen.

# MIDDAY

### A Reflection on Anxiety

It comes as an unpleasant surprise to many new parents to discover that anxiety is so much a part of parenthood. We expected to be so happy and here we are — worried!

Couples who have been parents several times usually worry less about the baby's crying, but let the baby get really sick and even veteran parents are afraid.

Anxiety is the negative side of many essential attitudes. In the case of child care, necessary attentiveness can expand into tension and worry. Many other desirable human traits run wild. For example, people who take work seriously may worry so much about it that they finally become unable to function effectively. Parenthood, then, is not the only place where we are anxious.

Being responsible for a small child reminds us that we cannot wholly control what happens. If we can face this we can cope with anxiety. There is no alternative to the anxiety of life except belief in the trustworthy God of Jesus.

This is not to say that there are no practical ways to deal with anxiety. To take every precaution for a child's safety is more likely to put our minds at rest than is carelessness. Anxiety is often caused by physical imbalances and is reinforced by exhaustion, particularly in a woman who has recently given birth. Parents of a newborn get really tired! There are forms of anxiety that should be treated medically. But neither medicine nor counseling can remove the risk at the heart of life and no responsible counselor tries to create the illusion that life without risk is possible. We must learn to deal head-on with anxiety.

Jesus reminds us that in the very midst of the tension of human life God has promised rest. "Rest" is a very important word in the Christian vocabulary. It is not merely an occasional break in the tiring daily struggle but God's response to anxiety.

### The Scriptures

Psalm 16. The psalmist celebrates his security in God.

Matt. 6:19–34. Jesus speaks to the problem of anxiety.

### A Prayer for the Hour

Blessed Father, we confess that we are not very experienced in coping with anxiety. Help us not to live in terror of what might happen but to entrust ourselves and our child (children) to you. Help us to accept the risk at the heart of life and to share the courage you revealed when you sent your Son to teach and save us. We want to learn to depend more on you. In Jesus' Name. Amen.

# EVENING

### A Theme for Meditation

My mouth shall praise thee . . . when I remember thee upon my bed, and meditate on thee in the night watches. Because thou hast been my help, therefore in the shadow of thy wings will I rejoice.

My soul followeth hard after thee: thy right hand
upholdeth thee.

(Ps. 63: 5, 6–8, KJV)

What goes on in our heads at night may well be
among the most important events of the day.
Those who have studied dreams know how dis-
closing they can be. Fears come to the surface in
symbolic forms. Scenes both violent and sometimes indescribably beautiful pass before us. When
we are troubled our dream life is especially active.

For parents repeatedly awakened by a newborn
child, nights are torn to remnants by the baby's
needs. To what do our minds turn when we are
half awake or dozing? Only too easily we can spin
scenarios that frighten us. We fall victim to anxiety
at a time when we are particularly vulnerable.

If we cannot control what comes into our minds,
at least we can decide what will be welcome there!
Our theme for meditation answers the tendency of
our imaginations to fall victim to the anxieties that
seize us in the darkness. "I think of you through the
watches of the night," says the psalmist. The God
of comfort, to whom Jesus prayed night after
night, awaits our prayers too.

## A Prayer for the Night

Now, O Lord, we commit ourselves and our baby
to you for the night. Do not let worries trouble our

dreams. When we are awakened, speak to us by your comforting presence. Reassure us that you care for us even more than we care for those we love best. Through Jesus we pray. Amen.

# DAY THREE
# *Courage*

## MORNING

### Adoration

You, O Lord, have blessed the house of your servant and it will be blessed forever!

(1 Chron. 17:27, NIV adapted)

### A Thought to Remember

In the Bible, the word "courage" has the meaning that we intend today when we say "heart": for example, "He has not the heart for the job!" The chronicler quotes King David as saying that he had found heart for prayer. "Your servant has found courage to pray to you." (1 Chron. 17:25)

Courage in the Bible is not heroism of the sort for which medals are awarded to soldiers. The Old Testament had its heroes; the Book of Judges records many heroic deeds. But physical courage gives way in the Bible to the quieter courage that everyone needs in order to live. Professor Tillich called it "the courage to be."

Sooner or later everyone experiences moments when the common burden of life seems just too great. Then we lose heart; "the courage to be" fails. What are we to do? We turn to God and we ask for courage to pray. To pray is to have the heart to go on; God gives the gift of courage for life. The believer affirms with David: "Your servant has found courage to pray to you."

### A Prayer for Courage

Dear Father, we confess that we have not yet learned how to cope with our fears. We have heard your Word but it takes root in us only very slowly, so that we easily fall into anxiety. Open our hearts to your promise that you will abide with us and give us the courage we need. In Christ we offer our prayer. Amen.

# MIDDAY

### A Reflection on Courage

Every day we read about children dying. Some of us have lost children of our own and we know the terror of losing another. The death of a child is all the more cruel because childhood seems very specially to belong to life. In the face of so many uncertainties it takes courage to bear and rear a child.

The Scriptures tell of divine interventions that preserved the lives of children. Infant Moses was doomed by Pharaoh's order; Jairus's twelve year old was dead when Jesus arrived. Both stories make a single point: God is supreme good, a victor over all evil designs and the cruelties of a world that is out of joint.

The joy of parenthood is tempered by many sobering reflections. The easy confidence of our youth is blown away by parenthood. We may wonder if we are adequate to the tests that lie ahead. Sometimes we feel outright panic.

It is a little hard to pull ourselves together just because some hearty optimist tells us to! Can we forget our fears by some act of will? Can we pretend that the dangers are not there? Can we stop looking at the nightly crime and arson news on the television? That might help!

The parents in today's Scriptures had the courage to face reality. Miriam did not pretend that her baby was not in danger. The danger was real and she took action. What courage it must have taken to launch her infant on the Nile in a tiny ark of basketwork! Grieved as he was, Jairus was not paralyzed by depression as he watched his daughter's health fail. He went to Jesus. Both these parents had lost control of the fate of their children yet they did not surrender. They entrusted their children to divine care.

This is the special courage that God offers parents: the courage to believe, to pray, and to act. The God of Miriam and Jairus waits for us.

### The Scriptures

Exod. 2:1–10. A baby is twice delivered.
Luke 8:40–56. A young girl is raised from death.

### A Prayer for the Hour

Heavenly Father, we thank you for the joy you have given us in the birth of our baby, in which you affirm life itself. We rejoice in all your gifts. Help us to entrust to your loving care all that means the most to us. Through your Son our Savior. Amen.

## EVENING

### A Theme for Meditation

"Stop wailing," Jesus said. "She is not dead but asleep."
(Luke 8:52, NIV)

Of course the child was dead! Everyone knew that! And the people laughed at Jesus.

Watch out for what "everyone knows!" Jesus spoke the truth in ways that made special demands on his listeners. His statement had two possible meanings. First, the child was alive and sleeping, the literal meaning. Because the bystanders thought no further they laughed at his ignorance. But he spoke with other intentions. He used the word "sleep" metaphorically to affirm that death cannot end life. Does not everyone awaken after sleep?

All too often we miss the second dimension of the words we hear. The disciples often did. How many times have we said of a statement, sometimes a child's, "Little did he know how truly he spoke." If we are alert to the second dimension we find larger meanings not only in words but also in events.

In how many ways Jesus forces us to expand our limited grasp of experiences we are sure we understand! To enter "into the mind of Christ" is to share his extraordinary insight into the meaning of the experiences that flow over us.

## A Prayer for the Night

Our Father in Heaven, we thank you for your kindness to us in assuring us of your care and for the gift of loving one another. Give us serenity when the night overtakes us. When we awaken to care for our baby, give us joy; when we are tired, grant us rest, and always lead us into your light. Through Jesus our Lord. Amen.

# DAY FOUR
## *Responsibility*

## MORNING

### Adoration

Alleluia! Salvation, and glory, and honour, and power, unto the Lord our God: for true and righteous are his judgments . . . Praise our God, all ye his servants, and ye that fear him, both small and great . . . Let us be glad and rejoice, and give honour to him.

(Rev. 19:1b, 5b, 7a, KJV)

### A Thought to Remember

We brought nothing into this world, and it is certain we can carry nothing out.

(1 Tim. 6:7, KJV)

The Bible often does not sound "religious" but simply practical! That is particularly true of the pastoral letters of St. Paul, which contain good advice on the practice of the Christian faith. Addressed to first century people and problems, they are remarkably relevant today.

The concern behind this little saying is how to relate love toward God to the responsibilities of providing the common necessities of food, clothing, and housing. St. Paul puts our concern for those necessities in perspective by reminding us that we both enter and leave the world empty-handed. The great questions of human life, such as where we are really headed, are virtually independent of possessions. The apostle's advice is: "If we have food and clothing we will be content with that." (1 Tim. 6:8, NIV)

St. Paul's attitude keeps anxiety in check. People who look to wealth have reason to be anxious. Wealth can vanish in a moment. The love of money diverts attention from what is really important. On the other hand, if "meeting your responsibilities" is never permitted to take over your life, you need never be afraid of possessions.

## A Prayer for Responsibility

Dear Father, when we look at the future of our child (children) we wonder if we have what it takes to carry such responsibility. There is so much that we cannot control! Give us courage. Show us that you are ready with special gifts for each day's tasks. Help us to recognize your loving presence and grant us your peace through Jesus Christ our Lord. Amen.

# MIDDAY

## A Reflection on Responsibility

We speak of "carrying responsibilities" as though it were a burden, and indeed it often is. We may love our jobs but we still have to get up in the dark, endure a certain amount of tedium, and cope with pressures. Young parents love their baby but when one of them must awaken at three a.m. to feed it, that is a burden.

The Bible is candid about this. Responsibility is often seen as a burden, and with good reason. In an agricultural society, such as that of Jesus' time, a year of abundance could be followed by hunger the next year, if harvests should fail. How were providers to feed their children? The western nations have few worries about food but there are new problems that we have created for ourselves, such as the spreading risks of pesticides and radioactivity. How can we improve our ability to respond to modern uncertainties?

Responsibility, understood in this way, is not so

much a burden as a qualification for survival. Is Jesus advocating irresponsibility when he says: "Take no thought for your life, what ye shall eat, or what ye shall drink"? (Matt. 6:25, KJV) Are we to be happy-go-lucky types? This is not what Jesus is saying! He is concerned with the problem of the "two masters." He continues: "Is not life more important than food, and the body more important than clothes?" (Matt. 6:25, NIV) It is a matter of the values by which life is to be organized and governed. Will we choose the urgent need of food, shelter, and clothing or the kingship of God?

Since we need both it seems extreme to pose this as a flat choice, but Jesus did exactly that. "You cannot serve God and mammon." The New Testament also says: "If any provide not for his own, and specially for those of his own house, he hath denied the faith, and is worse than an infidel." (1 Tim. 5:8, KJV)

The choice is not between holy negligence and sinful responsibility! (That was probably the misunderstanding with which St. Paul was dealing when he wrote to Timothy.) The question is: How can we be responsible people—responsible to our families and at the same time responsible to the supremacy of God in our lives? The kingdom of God is populated by citizens whose burdens and joys can never estrange them from the King. Quite the opposite! Every joy, every burden discloses the God of love in a new way.

## The Scriptures

Exod. 3 and 4:1–17. Moses is afraid to take the responsibility that God lays on him, and God responds.

Matt. 6:24–34. Does Jesus reject responsible behavior?

## A Prayer for the Hour

Dear Father, we want to know how to be truly responsible not only to our child (children) but also to you. Give us a trustworthy sense of what is really important; teach us what is not important at all. Do not let us be pulled apart by forces that we cannot reconcile. Let your Lordship stand at the center for us. In Jesus' Name. Amen.

# EVENING

## A Theme for Meditation

Therefore do not worry about tomorrow, for tomorrow will worry about itself. Each day has enough trouble of its own.

(Matt. 6:34, NIV)

"Sufficient unto the day is the evil thereof," wrote

the sixteenth-century Englishman who translated this saying from the Greek. Today we might say: "One day at a time! Don't borrow tomorrow's trouble." If every day has its own troubles, Christ has also declared that his grace is sufficient. We are in the situation of the Hebrews in the desert. God fed them but only one day at a time. If they tried to store the manna it rotted. He forced them to trust him all over again each day. Every morning he was waiting for them.

Our ability to respond to the great possibilities of each new day depends largely on our trust that he awaits us with strength for the day. God is not against planning ahead! That is one of the responsibilities of life. But no matter how thorough our plans, we cannot control many of the circumstances that affect us. So we try to live in trust.

## A Prayer for the Night

Blessed God, the work of the day is done and we commit it to you. Where we have responded in love, we thank you. Where we have done evil, we ask your forgiveness. Where we have been insensitive, awaken us. You have given the night for rest but we are restless. Rescue us from anxiety so that our hearts may be yours. When our baby awakens give us patience, through our Lord, Jesus Christ. Amen.

# DAY FIVE
## *Promise*

## MORNING

### Adoration

Praise be to the Lord, the God of Israel, because he has come and has redeemed his people. He has raised up a horn of salvation for us . . . to remember his holy covenant.

(Luke 1:68, 69a, 72b, NIV)

### A Thought to Remember

"Wait for the promise of the Father."

Every culture takes form around great basic ideas that distinguish it from other cultures. We are formed by these ideas. Once a culture begins to doubt its basic ideas, it is on the road to dissolution. Socrates shook early Greek culture and religion to its foundations by his questions and the

Athenians were so profoundly disturbed that they executed him on a charge of corrupting their young people.

One formative idea of the Hebrew and Christian tradition is the *covenant:* God's trustworthy promise to guide history and humankind to his own goals. The Bible teaches us to be sensitive to the workings of God in the world and in ourselves. Prophets risked their lives when they boldly told kings that God's ways were not their ways and that they would bring the people to ruin unless they kept the covenant.

When times are difficult it is sometimes not easy to see the work of God in what is happening. How do we deal with this?

"Wait for the promise of the Father," replies Jesus. "Wait" does not mean "kick your heels" like the paralyzed characters in *Waiting for Godot* or "tap your toe" with impatience but rather "be attentive to." We are to examine all that goes on in the light of the promise of God. "Watch and wait," said Jesus, "for he comes just when you least expect him."

## A Prayer for the Divine Promise

Father in Heaven, we accept responsibility for the young life that you have entrusted to us and we ask your help. Give us fresh understanding of your gifts and promises. We commit ourselves and our child to you. Renew your promises to us, dear Father, for Jesus Christ's sake. Amen.

# MIDDAY

### A Reflection on Promise

For Christians the fabric of life is woven of promises. The Old Testament is the story of the unfolding of God's promises in the life of his people. Even secular relationships are governed by promises. Business contracts, oaths in the courtroom, credit cards, home loans, wills, and marriages are all promises. There is considerable debate today about the bonds that bring people together in society. We hear of marriage contracts drawn up before a wedding.

Marriage is particularly damaged by failure to understand it as a covenant. How often we hear a divorced person say of a former spouse: "He no longer met my needs," or "I just outgrew her." For persons who regard marriage as a binding covenant these problems do not justify divorce. If marriage is merely an arrangement to meet one's needs, it may be rightly abandoned when the needs of one of the partners change.

The power of a covenant in the presence of God

to sustain marriage is unique to believers. The only justification for divorce in traditional Hebrew and Christian communities is infidelity, which simply means "promise breaking."

To bear a child is to enter into a new covenant with God on behalf of the child. The ceremonies that Christians celebrate with their infants — dedication, baptism, christening — are times when parents and the members of the congregations both make promises and are reminded of God's promises. Our relationship to our children is no longer defined solely by our feelings or theirs but by a holy covenant.

The solemnity of these promises adds seriousness to marriage itself. Marriages do not achieve maturity without work and sometimes suffering, nor are children brought to adulthood without sacrifice. The history of God's covenant with the Hebrew people is strewn with broken promises, rejection, and willful disobedience. But God always reaches out to his people, rebuking them and punishing their infidelities, forgiving and never abandoning them.

That is the model by which we live in both marriage and parenthood. Christ is Spirit and his Spirit abides with us to help us keep our promises, or if we fail, to find our way back to him and to one another.

## The Scriptures

Gen. 17:1–8. Jer. 31:31–34. God makes his promises.

Luke 1:67–79. The father of John the Baptist salutes Jesus.

## A Prayer for the Hour

God our Father, we confess that we would lose our way without you. We would not know right from wrong, nor could we tell good from bad without your holy law. Open our hearts to your gospel so that we may willingly love your Son, who so greatly loved us that he submitted to injustice, disgrace and death for our sakes. Through him we pray. Amen.

# EVENING

## A Theme for Meditation

Through his great and precious promises you may participate in the divine nature.

(2 Pet. 1:3, 4, NIV adapted)

The highest possibility for human existence is to enter into the very being of God. This is to have the ability to know God. It is only "natural," we are accustomed to say, to respond to our life experience with desire in one of its many forms: greed, sexual feeling, love of power, or pride of status. But if that is natural, it flows from a nature sick with self-concern.

An altogether different kind of nature awaits us. There is a whole range of behavior that flows spontaneously from the divine nature. God responds to us — and if we share his nature we may respond to him and other people — with love instead of desire. There is only one right object of desire: God himself, arousing in us the desire to be like him, to know him as he is, to love as he loves. How can we be like that?

"Through his great and precious promises you may participate in the divine nature."

### A Prayer for the Night

Heavenly Father, our nights mean more to us than they did before our baby was born. We need to rest and we need to love him (her) more when our rest is interrupted. When we awaken in the night, be present with us. Let our care for the baby express our response to your love. In Jesus' Name. Amen.

# DAY SIX
## *Joy*

## MORNING

### Adoration

To him who is able to keep you from falling and to present you before his glorious presence without fault and with great joy — to the only God our Savior be glory, majesty, power and authority, through Jesus Christ our Lord, before all ages, now and forevermore. Amen.

(Jude 24, NIV)

### A Thought to Remember

A young mother may wonder how she can feel joyful after spending the night catnapping between feedings. Joy is not the same as pleasant physical sensations, such as feeling relaxed and rested. The joy of parents cannot depend on that! Its source lies deeper. It is simply the child's presence that gives them joy.

Anyone who has lost a child knows the anguish of that child's sudden absence. What had been an engrossing presence is gone and the emptiness fairly burns with pain.

Joy flows from presence. Joy is fullness; it is a sign of purpose achieved. The joy of being married flows from loving and being loved by another who is continually present. Beyond all ordinary fulfillments, beyond the presence of husband, wife, or child is the largest presence of all: God with us. The Bible gives God-as-present with us a special name: Emmanuel.

The writer of Psalm 16 is not speaking of the perishable joy of human existence, so early turned to grief by the loss of loved ones. He sings of the imperishable joy of the divine presence. "You will fill me with joy in your presence." (Ps. 16:11b, NIV)

## A Prayer for Joy

Heavenly Father, we are grateful that we can greet this day with joy. We thank you for our baby and for every good thing that his (her) birth means to us. Give us heart for today's tasks. Grant us wisdom to care for this new soul whom you have entrusted to us. Through our joy in our baby awaken in us the joy of your own presence. Through our Lord, Jesus Christ. Amen.

# MIDDAY

## A Reflection on Joy

Our language is rich in words that denote strong and deeply rooted emotion. There are good words, of course, that speak very mildly. "Nice," for example, is a positive word but not especially strong. What would you think of a young father who would say: "Yes, this is a nice baby!" Or "pleasant" or "amusing." "No more than that?" we might ask.

Babies are not always pleasant and when they have grown into adolescents they may be downright disagreeable at times. But we are not bonded to our children because they are nice or agreeable. It is a matter of love and love is not anchored in soft ground. It holds firm in high winds.

"Joy," like "love," is a strong word. The two are akin. There can be no true joy without love. Joy is an expression of love. When love speaks, there is always joy in its voice. Is there any word more joyous than the simple phrase, "I love you"?

When we speak of "inner joy" we do not mean that it flourishes in human solitude but rather that joy is lastingly rooted in our inner life. But joy, like love, is directed toward others. It is joy *in another* before it is a personal feeling of joy. Joy, unlike happiness, can exist along with grief and pain. St. Paul says that Jesus, "for the joy that was set before him endured the cross." Jesus so greatly loved us that he actually found joy in finishing the painful, necessary work of the cross. It was *our* presence that gave his death joy for him. How far from happiness the cross was!

If Jesus endured the cross in the fullness of joy, we can love, we can even be joyous without happy feelings.

### The Scriptures

Psalm 51:1–12. King David celebrates the joy of his forgiveness.

John 16:19–24. Jesus promises that joy will follow grief.

### A Prayer for the Hour

Blessed Father, we are grateful for your gift of joy. We are not always joyous! We know emptiness, uncertainty, and disappointment. But now we are discovering joy in a new way. Help us to understand the signs of your presence, offering us the fullness of your own joy. Let our baby bless us. In Christ we pray. Amen.

# EVENING

## A Theme for Meditation

> Even though you do not see him now, you believe in him and are filled with inexpressible and glorious joy.
>
> (1 Pet. 1:8, NIV)

Not everyone who is present is visible! Memory enables us to know people as present in a certain way, even in their physical absence. We do not see Jesus with our eyes, but he is present in ways that go beyond remembering. The Holy Spirit is an active power within the community of believers and within each of us. The joy of believers remembering the painful labor of Christ for us is evidence of the divine Spirit abiding in us. The joyous celebration of the Sacrament of the Lord's Supper not only recalls the Savior ("Do this in remembrance of me") but also marks his active presence ("Behold, I am with you always") by his Spirit ("whom the Father will send in my Name").

Joy is our response to the great deeds of God in the past and also to his promises for the future. Although not present as he was with his disciples, Jesus comes to us through his living Spirit and at length, at the end of the age, he himself comes. The people of God therefore look to the future with joy, not with fear. It is not true that the future holds nothing but threats of broken health and nuclear war! We may live with joy in expectation of our Lord's coming again.

## A Prayer for the Night

Dear Father, we confess that we are filled with wonder at all that is happening. The coming of this baby is more than we knew! Let our joy in this child lead us into your presence. Help us to learn to love you more dearly as we respond to our baby's need. Grant us joy in one another and be present to show us all your ways. Through Christ our Lord. Amen.

# DAY SEVEN
## *Love*

## MORNING

### Adoration

In the beginning was the Word. . . . Through him all things were made. . . . In him was life, and that life was the light of men. The light shines in the darkness. . . . The true light that gives light to every man was coming into the world.

(John 1:1–9, NIV selected)

### A Thought to Remember

It is easy to become sentimental when speaking of love. St. Paul is very far from that when he reflects on love! And St. John wrote: "This is how we know what love is: Jesus Christ laid down his life for us." (1 John 3:16a, NIV) Divine love was born into the world in the catastrophe of the cross! It is powerful and it compels us.

Parents know how love compels. What normal adult does not react when a baby cries? Parental caring impels us to respond.

The human spirit that has turned toward God is profoundly moved by God's great acts of love. "He died for all, that those who live should no longer live for themselves but for him who died for them and was raised again." (2 Cor. 5:15) Obviously, not everyone is moved by the death of Christ. Nor is everyone moved by the suffering of the world's children. A person who is preoccupied with self is insensitive to the agonies of others and cannot love.

Many eyes look but do not see. Once our eyes are opened, we see at Calvary something more than one among many grievous events. We see God's love and after that, "Christ's love compels us."

### A Prayer for Love

Loving Father, we praise you for your great love for us. Let your love uphold us when our feelings of love fail us. Help us to live so that our baby may grow up to know you. If bad feelings sometimes spoil our caring, show our child (children) that your love restores us. Through our Lord Jesus Christ. Amen.

# MIDDAY

### A Reflection on Love

Love is not something that exists independently of human beings, like a rock which would be there even if people were not. Love is something that someone does.

We perhaps assume that God's love is the name of his attitude toward us. That is not altogether wrong but it falls short of the larger meaning of divine love.

God himself is love; not only his attitude or his relationships. It is we who think of love as an attitude. A person may have a given attitude — or not have it! Attitudes are not the same as persons. For example, we may believe we should have natural feelings of love for our child (children). But new parents are often disappointed because they do not feel great warm surges of love for their new baby. The truth is that bonding develops gradually in parents as well as in children. We have very little experience that prepares us to understand divine love.

We can see the sense in giving up our life for the sake of a good person or perhaps even a baby. But why would anyone do that for a person who cares nothing whatever for him? Yet "while we were yet sinners"—while we were totally uncaring and not loving at all—"Christ died for us." God here discloses the difference between his loving and ours.

Love is not like pleasure or disappointment. Feelings and moods disappear after a while. The love that is God's lives in a totally changed human personality. We commonly speak of sexual activity as "making love" and it truly can be—but not unless more than sexual desire is present. Sexual excitement subsides, but love abides. If sex is to be a loving thing, something that outlives it must be joined with it.

Love is nothing less than the very being of God. To know God is to know love. There is no way to know love except to know God first. God so desires us to share his love that he gave his beloved Son to die for us.

To understand how Christ's dying works to save us—to know exactly what "for us" means—is less important than to respond to it. If we hear God's great "I love you," we have understood the atonement and we reply: "Make me free to love you, O Lord!"

Sex, childbearing, and parenthood are the materials of love, but yet not love. Without love these have no soul. Evil spirits of jealousy and envy often inhabit human relationships. Family life that is a dwelling place of God's love must draw from its source.

We teach love to our child (children) by our own acts of love. But love does not reside solely in correct behavior. It is something we *are*. We must *be* love.

How is it possible to love wife or husband? To love your baby?

Love is possible because we are offered a new personhood. "In Christ all things are made new," wrote St. Paul. When Christ dwells in us, a new parenthood is possible, parenthood grounded in faith.

Just to give birth does not guarantee that a mother will love her baby. But to embrace God's Son is to be in touch with supreme love. His new people can begin to love as God loves us.

## The Scriptures

Hos. 2:14–23. The prophet speaks of God's determination to recover the love of his unfaithful people.
1 John 4:7–21. Life in the love that God gives.

## A Prayer for the Hour

Dear Father, we confess our desire to live in your love by calling you Father. Help us to love our child (children) as you do. Help us to love without asking anything in return. Transform us, dear Father, for we are not yet that kind of person! Change us! We cannot know love or be love without you. Through our Lord Jesus. Amen.

# EVENING

## A Theme for Meditation

Love never fails.

(1 Cor. 13:8 NIV)

If love and God are the same, love cannot fail. For love to fail, God would have to die—but God is life itself. Love abides when everything else withers.

Every broken marriage, every estrangement of parents from children testifies that human love as we know it does not abide. Yet the love of a mother for her child, although less than God's love, opens her to a real person other than herself. A baby can break the iron ring of self-love. Young married people may have given their whole attention to one another but no longer! Both may resent this! A new personhood is forced on them and they can fail.

The love that is God does not fail. Faith itself is not God. Our trust can fail. Hope is not God; our hope can fail. But love is God's before it is ours. If our feelings of love chill, God remains unchanged.

How shall we be faithful to our children? There is a way! Let the love that is granted to us through Jesus come to us and abide within us. That sort of love does not fail.

## A Prayer for the Night

We thank you, blessed Father, for the day now ending. Show us all the loving ways you have come to us today. If we are occupied with our own feelings, liberate us; if we do not perceive the needs of those we love, make us attentive. Let all we do for ourselves and others honor you; through Jesus our Lord. Amen.

# Additional Prayers and Blessings

## PRAYERS

### For Freedom to Pray

Dear Father, take our minds for your own. Let us not feel hurried by the day's tasks. Help us to overcome distraction. Give something of your own holiness to ordinary duties and send your Holy Spirit to us. Through Jesus we pray. Amen.

### For the Light of Your Presence

Heavenly Father, we are not expert at living in two kingdoms! We are easily overwhelmed by the concerns of daily life and forget that the spirit you created in us longs for you. Give us just enough of the good things of physical life to be free of worry. Free us for yourself. We know we cannot live by bread alone. Nourish us by the Word that comes from you. In Jesus' Name. Amen.

### For Self-acceptance

Dear Father, we sometimes have feelings that are too big for us. We do not know how to express them and they almost make us afraid. Help us to accept ourselves and to understand what we are becoming. Teach us to love one another beyond all approving or liking. Grant us joy to endure through Jesus our Lord. Amen.

### For Courage to Trust

Blessed Father, we need to learn courage from the parents of the Bible. Give us heart to trust, to pray, and to act even when we are afraid. Teach us to walk with confidence in your holy path. In the Name of Jesus our Lord. Amen.

### For Freedom from Fear

We are grateful, dear Lord, for our joy in being parents and for the means to care for our child (children). We ask you not to permit our fears to throw shadows on our love for our baby and for each other. Show us how to rest in you. Through our Lord Jesus. Amen.

### For Renewal

Blessed God, we greet your gift of a new day with joy! If we have carried yesterday's irritations through the night, forgive us. If fatigue threatens to dull the day's beginning, refresh us! Grant us courage to hope in things that abide. In Jesus' Name. Amen.

# BLESSINGS

## Upon Mothers

Blessed is she who has believed that what the Lord has said to her will be accomplished.

(Luke 1:45, NIV)

## Upon Children

Let the little children come to me, and do not hinder them, for the kingdom of God belongs to such as these.

(Luke 18:16, NIV)

## Upon the Joyous

As the Father has loved me, so have I loved you. Now remain in my love. If you obey my commands, you will remain in my love . . . I have told you this so that my joy may be in you and that your joy may be complete.

(John 15:9, 10a, 11, NIV)

## Upon Witnesses

Ye are the light of the world. A city that is set on an hill cannot be hid. . . . Let your light so shine before men that they may see your good works and glorify your Father which is in heaven.

(Matt. 5:14, 16, KJV)

## Upon the Forgiven

May God himself, the God of peace, sanctify you through and through. May your whole spirit, soul and body be kept blameless at the coming of our Lord Jesus Christ.

(1 Thess. 5:23, NIV)

## Upon the Obedient

I am Alpha and Omega, the beginning and the end, the first and the last. Blessed are they that do his commandments, that they may have right to the tree of life, and may enter in through the gates into the city.

(Rev. 22:13, 14, KJV)

## Upon All Who Trust

Find rest, O my soul, in God alone; my hope comes from him. . . . He is my fortress, I will not be shaken.

(Ps. 62:5, 6, NIV)